**Second Edition copyrighted 2(**

*Fresh Eggs*

Written by Greg Verga
Illustrated by James Balkovek

©Copyright September 1, 2011

Library of Congress 2011939541

Printed in the US

Publisher Wiggles Press, Cambridge, Massachusetts

Book Designed by Rochelle O'Neal Thorpe

Wiggles Press Publishing, Inc.

**wigglespress.com**

*Dedicated to our new addition, Cameron Joseph Ragusa*

*For Kellie, Abbie, Patrick and Julia - always my inspiration;
and to our beloved Nana Martin for her encouragement.*

One Saturday morning in spring I awoke to the sound of hammering. The noise was coming from Daddy.

He was building something.

I quickly got dressed, got my tools, and ran outside so I could help.

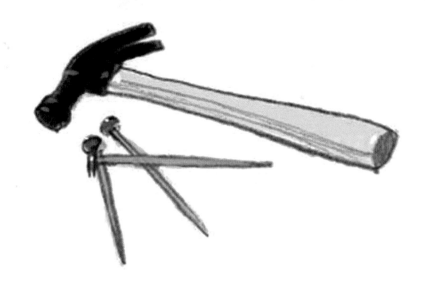

I came running over to him and asked,
"What are you making?"

"I'm building a chicken coop, that's a little
house that chickens live in."

"Why?"

"So we can have fresh eggs every day," he said.
"Do you want to help?"

"Sure."

So Daddy showed me what to do.  I held the nails
for him, handed him his tools and he even let me use
the screwdriver.

We would build a little bit every day when Daddy came home from work.

Then one day he said, "We have just about finished. . . It's ready for the chickens."

I was puzzled. "Where will we get the chickens?"

"I ordered some from the hatchery."

"What's a hatchery?"

"That's a place that hatches eggs," he told me. "A mother hen hatches her eggs by sitting on them to keep them warm. In a hatchery they have big machines called incubators that keep the eggs warm."

The next day we got into the car and  drove to the hatchery.
When we got there Daddy held my hand.

"I want you to see something."

We went into a room.  It was very warm. There was a
big box there with glass windows on the sides.

Daddy held me up to see.  At first I saw a lot of eggs.
Then I looked again and I saw some fuzzy yellow chicks!

Daddy pointed to an egg with a hole in it.
"There's a baby chick in there trying to get out.
He uses his beak to poke through the shell."

We watched for a while and I could see a little beak popping through the shell.

Finally the top of the shell was off and the little chick wriggled his way out. He was all wet and wobbly.

Daddy said that the chick was covered with down. It would soon dry, his legs would get stronger and he would begin to cheep and walk around with the other chicks.

A man walked over to Daddy carrying a box with holes on the sides.

"Come on," said Daddy as he took the box.

When I got into the car Daddy buckled me in and put the box on my lap.

I peeked through one of the holes.

It was filled with fuzzy yellow chicks!

When we got home Daddy opened the door of the little house we made. It was warm in there too, just like at the hatchery.

Since we didn't have a mother hen we would use a big red light hanging from the ceiling. The light bulb was very hot and it kept the room just right for the chicks.

Every day we would check to make sure the chicks were alright. We had a little tray we kept their food on and a little bowl for their water.

The little yellow chicks seemed to grow every day. After a few weeks little feathers were on their wings. Eventually the feathers replaced all of their down.

When summer began Daddy took the big red light bulb out. He said that they could stay warm enough on their own.

We had done a lot of work and our little chicks had grown into big chickens, but they hadn't given us one egg.

"I thought we got the chickens for eggs, Daddy and they haven't given us any."

"They will soon enough and there's just one more thing we have to do."

He went into the shed and came out with a wooden box. Inside the box he put some straw.

"This is a nest box; it's where the chickens will lay their eggs," he said as he nailed the box to the wall inside the chicken coop.

"They like a soft and dark place to lay their eggs."

Every morning when I woke up I would run out to check for eggs, but every day was the same – nothing!

By the end of the summer I was thinking that it would never happen, but it did.

I was doing my morning egg check and there it was. It was a tiny brown egg!

I picked it up very carefully and carried it into the house.

I could hardly wait for Daddy to get home from work.

Finally I heard the front door open. I grabbed our little egg and ran to see Daddy.

He was as excited as I was. He even took a picture of me holding our first egg.

That night at supper Daddy and I shared the world's smallest omelet and it was yummy!

# Fresh Eggs Glossary

Chicken Coop - a small house for chickens

Hatchery - a place for hatching eggs

Incubator - An apparatus where the temperature can be controlled for growing and hatching eggs

Down - the soft first feathers of young birds

Brood - to warm, protect or cover young birds

Nest box - a box in a chicken coop for chickens to lay their eggs

*Artist, James Balkovek*

An illustrator for 30 years, James Balkovek has illustrated hundreds of educational and children's books. His career has spanned the fields of advertising illustration, graphic design, trade and children's illustration, educational publishing and teaching. Currently residing in Indiana with his wife and their menagerie of pets, he enjoys painting, reading, and travel.

*Greg Verga*

This Story is the first book written by Greg Verga.

He lives in Gloucester, Massachusetts with his wife Kellie.
He has three grown children – Abbie; Patrick and Julia.

Abbie is married to Stephen and this new Edition of Fresh Eggs is
dedicated to their new addition – their new grandson – Cameron Joseph.

The family is rounded out by Dan the Dachshund and Lilly the cat along
with a flock of chickens and guinea hens.

Greg is looking forward to teaching Cameron all about raising chickens.

By day Greg is a real estate broker and by night a songwriter/bass
player with Black Sheep Stampede - an indie rock band.

Made in the USA
Middletown, DE
30 December 2022

20701644R00015